THE SMOKIN' BOOK OF CIGAR BOX

ART & DESIGNS

THE Smokin' BOOK OF
CIGAR BOX
ART & DESIGNS

MORE THAN 100 OF THE BEST LABELS FROM THE JOHN & CAROLYN GROSSMAN COLLECTION

JOHN GROSSMAN

FOX CHAPEL
PUBLISHING

DEDICATED TO CAROLYN GROSSMAN

Text and illustrations © 2012 John Grossman

© 2012 Fox Chapel Publishing Company, Inc.
The Smokin' Book of Cigar Box Art & Designs is an original work, first published in 2012
by Fox Chapel Publishing Company, Inc., East Petersburg, PA.

ISBN 978-1-56523-546-5

Edited by: Katie Weeber
Designed by: Jason Deller

Library of Congress Cataloging-in-Publication Data

Grossman, John.
   The smokin' book of cigar box art & designs / John Grossman.
      pages cm
   Includes index.
   ISBN 978-1-56523-546-5
   1. Cigar box labels--United States. 2. Grossman, John--Art collections. 3. Grossman, Carolyn--Art
collections. I. Title.
   NC1883.6.U6G765 2012
   741.6'920973--dc23
                              2012011000

To learn more about the other great books from Fox Chapel Publishing, or to find a retailer near you,
call toll-free 800-457-9112 or visit us at *www.FoxChapelPublishing.com*.

Note to Authors: We are always looking for talented authors to write new books. Please send a brief
letter describing your idea to Acquisition Editor, 1970 Broad Street, East Petersburg, PA 17520.

Printed in China
First printing

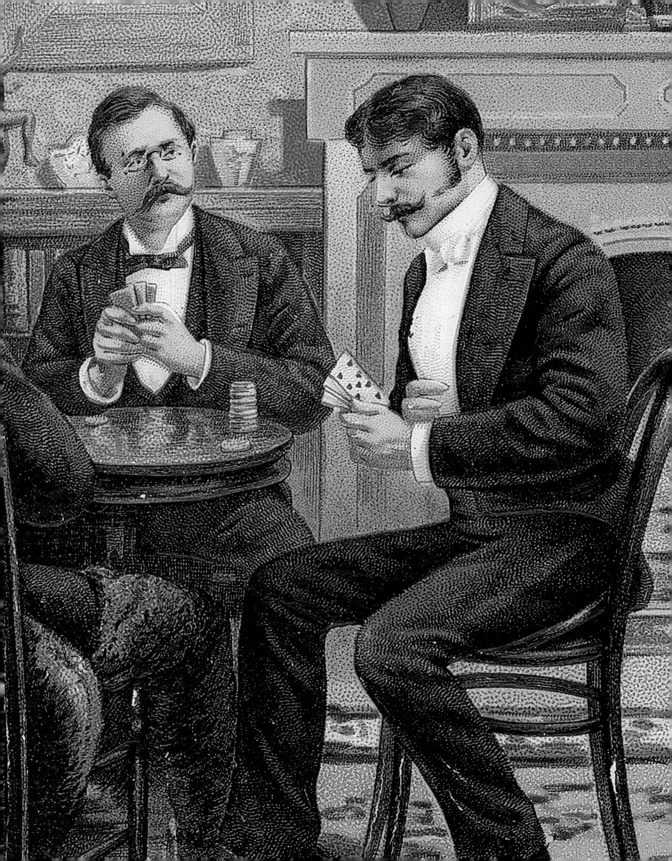

CONTENTS

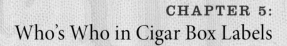 

INTRODUCTION

The amusing and slightly risqué situation shown here presents a subject thought likely to appeal to male cigar smokers. Label created circa 1880–1889.

In 1492, Columbus discovered the cigar. Two of his sailors were sent ashore on a reconnaissance mission to what is now Cuba. They reported back that the natives wrapped certain fragrant dried leaves in palm or maize, somewhat like a musket formed of paper, lighted one end and inhaled the smoke through the other.

Columbus took samples back to Spain, where one of his sailors, Rodrigo de Jerez, continued to smoke tobacco in public, and was rewarded with three years imprisonment. Eventually, inevitably, the habit took hold among the privileged classes first, because of the high cost of tobacco. By the eighteenth century, cigar smoking had spread through much of the Western world, including the American colonies. Israel Putnam, future general of Revolutionary War fame, brought three

donkey loads of Havana cigars to Connecticut from George III's war on Cuba in 1762. So began New England's long cigar tradition, subsequently championed by John Quincy Adams, a connoisseur of Havana cigars.

The acceptance of cigars as a smoking novelty grew slowly in America during fifty years (1762–1810), taking another fifty years to become accepted form (1810–1860), and then gaining full momentum during and after the Civil War. Victorians everywhere lit up in emulation of famous cigar smokers Ulysses S. Grant and Mark Twain. Novelist and early feminist George Sand was the most noted woman cigar smoker in the Victorian age. Rosa Bonheur, the French animal painter, also smoked cigars.

For fifty years after that, the cigar reigned supreme. In the 1870s and 1880s, no man considered himself well dressed without a cigar. By 1900, four out of five men were said to smoke cigars, with 20,000 cigar factories scattered throughout the nation to supply them. In 1907, cigar sales peaked in the United States—eighty-six per capita. Out of every dollar spent on tobacco products, sixty cents went for cigars.

With four out of five men smoking cigars, cigar companies began to pour money into advertising, seeking to attract customers with bright, colorful designs that included the images thought most likely to appeal to cigar smokers. Thousands of designs were created, and millions of labels were printed, featuring such subject matter as alluring women, sports, presidential campaigns, popular individuals and literary characters, tobacco plantations, transportation vehicles, animals, cartoon characters, foreign subjects, and historical eras.

Without the development of lithography and chromolithography as printing technologies, however, producing these labels would have been impossible. For centuries, letterpress relief printing and intaglio (printing from incised or engraved metal plates) were the most common printing methods. Prints created using these methods could be produced only in black and white, however. Color could be added by hand after printing, but this was expensive. In 1800, fine, colored engravings could still only be afforded by the well to do. All this changed after the invention of lithography in Bavaria, Germany, in 1798 by Alois Senefelder. Senefelder's lithography process combined surface printing from stones with the mutual repellence of water and greasy substances. In lithography, an image is drawn on a stone with a greasy ink substance called tusche, and a thin layer of water is applied to the blank or non-printing areas of the stone. When printing ink is added to the stone, it is attracted to the tusche and repelled by the water. The image is transferred to paper and run through a press under pressure to produce a mirror image.

Lithography stones and the images drawn on them facilitated the rapid production of multiple identical prints. This 1866 stone for a Barbour's Standard Thread label has the image incised into the stone in the manner of traditional engraving rather than drawn on the surface of the stone as in the regular lithographic process.

The lithography process revolutionized the printing industry, but lithographic prints were first printed in black and white. Color might be added by hand after printing, but was not part of the printing process. It was only after the process of chromolithography was developed that full color printing became a viable option. This 1873 print is titled *Central Park, N. Y. The First Ride.* Courtesy of the Library of Congress.

CENTRAL PARK, N.Y.

The first ride.

In 1837, French printer Godefroy Engelmann developed a method for printing in multiple colors from stones—what is referred to today as chromolithography. By the 1860s, the commercial chromolithographic process had been perfected, making printed color inexpensive and pervasive. People couldn't get enough of it. Companies scrambled to take advantage of it in their advertising and promotions, including cigar companies seeking to promote one of the era's most popular products. By the end of the century, lush, full color chromolithographed pictures, some even embossed and die cut, were being given away free as advertising promotions by merchants and manufacturers. The labels on boxes of 5¢ cigars were commonly printed in ten colors, gilded and embossed, on high-quality, clay-coated paper stock.

America's nascent lithographic industry benefited substantially from an influx of German emigrants already well trained in the craft, who were attracted by the much higher wages and better trade opportunities than those offered in their homeland. George Schlegel (1819–1883) was one such emigrant, and the company he founded in 1849 participated in the expansion of the new industry in America. Carried on by his heirs, three men all named George Schlegel, the George Schlegel Lithographic Company remained a family owned business until 1958, when it merged with another company. In the late 1870s the company began keeping samples of its works, resulting in a vast collection of cigar box labels (the company's primary product) that records more than eighty years of commercial lithographic work.

Chromolithography required up to ten stones to print multiple layers of transparent color inks on a sheet of paper, resulting in a color image. This photo shows the original lithographic stone drawing used to print the pink color layer of an *El Trelles* cigar box label.

The *El Trelles* keyline shows the non-printing line art applied to each original stone as a guide to the artist for shapes and color patterns.

The following images show each individual layer of color used to create the final *El Trelles* label. This is the yellow layer.

Dark red *El Trelles* layer.

Dark brown *El Trelles* layer.

Light brown *El Trelles* layer.

Dark blue *El Trelles* layer.

Light blue *El Trelles* layer.

Buff (flesh tone) *El Trelles* layer.

Gold (gold bronzing powder) *El Trelles* layer.

Pink *El Trelles* layer. This layer would have been printed using the stone shown on page 11.

Gray *El Trelles* layer. Gray was one of the last colors applied in the printing sequence and was typically used to tone other colors printed previously that appeared too strong.

The combination of colored layers shown on pages 11 and 12 resulted in this beautiful *El Trelles* label. Schlegel office file copy, 1936. The J. C. Newman Cigar Company now owns the *El Trelles* brand.

ABOUT THE JOHN AND CAROLYN GROSSMAN COLLECTION

The largest holdings of the Schlegel archive are part of a special collection in The John and Carolyn Grossman Collection, one of the world's largest collections of printed ephemera. The collection comprises approximately 250,000 items and contains labels documenting the development of the lithography and chromolithography process from circa 1820 to 1920.

The collection was started in 1974 when John Grossman purchased several printed ephemera pieces from an antiques store in Port Costa, California. Those few pieces quickly multiplied to become a collection of thousands of printed ephemera items.

As described by E. Richard McKinstry, Library Director and Andrew W. Mellon Senior Librarian at Winterthur Museum, Garden & Library in his foreword to *Labeling America*:

> The numerous and varied items and images to be found in the [John and Carolyn Grossman] collection include Christmas, Valentine, and greeting cards; children's toys, books, and amusements; postcards and scrapbooks; product boxes; and textile samples, among many others—all portraying the customs, attitudes, and ideals of Victorian and Edwardian life. Among the collection's treasures are the first commercially produced Christmas card (1843), its accompanying printer's proof, an American Christmas card from about 1850, and an incredible 41-pound album that commemorates the Golden Jubilee of Queen Victoria's reign with thousands of chromolithographs of English life.

German emigrant George Schlegel founded George Schlegel Lithographic Company in 1849. The company would help shape America's lithographic industry and produce thousands of chromolithographic labels for cigars and other products.

Among the collection's contents are more than 80,000 cigar box labels and related cigar items from cigar companies in America, Cuba, Canada, and Europe. A particularly special item is a box containing 50 cigars featuring images of the country's first 26 presidents on their bands. Labels from the George Schlegel Lithographic Company make up a large portion of the cigar-related items found in the collection, and it is from The John and Carolyn Grossman Collection that the cigar box labels featured in this book were selected. The reader will note that while the George Schlegel Lithographic Company produced most of the labels shown, those produced by other nineteenth and twentieth century companies are also included.

The John and Carolyn Grossman collection is housed at Winterthur Museum, Garden & Library in Wilmington, Delaware. More striking images of artifacts from the collection can be found in John Grossman's book, *Labeling America*.

1

THE WILD, WILD WEST

The nineteenth century in American history is marked by a steady expansion into the western half of the United States. This expansion led to numerous historical events and advancements, such as the war with Mexico (1846–1848), the 1849 gold rush, the development of the Pony Express, and the construction of the Transcontinental Railroad. The American cowboy became a popular figure in households across the country, and stories of conflict between the U.S. army and Native Americans in western states became matters of national interest. With this intense focus on the Western United States, it is no surprise cigar box labels picked up Western themes, featuring images from cowboys and Native Americans to gold prospectors and the American Bison.

Charles Marion Russell (1864–1926), also known as the "cowboy artist," was an artist of the old American West. He created more than 2,000 paintings of cowboys, Indians, and western landscapes, as well as bronze sculptures. He signed his works "CM Russell". Given his volume of work, his appearance on this 1902 label is not surprising.

CHAS. M. RUSSELL

"THE COWBOY ARTIST."

COL. CODY

Popularly known as Buffalo Bill, William Frederick Cody (1846–1917) served as an army scout and cavalryman. He eventually entered show business, organizing and performing plays with a Wild West theme. He formed the Buffalo Bill Combination, which performed "Buffalo Bill's Wild West" until 1913. The show featured authentic cowboy and Native American performers, as well as live western animals. Label created circa 1900–1909.

While the text on this label indicates the man is on his way to the Klondike gold rush in Skagway, Alaska, in 1896, the central figure is actually copied from an 1850 Currier and Ives print, *An Independent Gold Hunter on His Way to California*. Office album file copy, W.K. Gresh & Son, July 11, 1898.

INDIAN SQUAW

LITHO. GEO. SCHLEGEL 136 A 140 CENTRE ST. NEW YORK.

TRADE MARK REGISTERED.

A pretty Indian maid gives this circa 1890–1899 label a strong Western theme and marks the association of the American Indian with tobacco.

SPEARSMAN

TITLE & DESIGN REGISTERED.

A cigar manufacturer in Buffalo, New York, selected this powerful Native American portrait to be the image of the Spearsman cigar on this circa 1910–1919 label.

19

The buffalo, more correctly called the American Bison, is an iconic Western symbol. Bison once roamed the country's grasslands in massive herds and are the largest extant land animals in North America. Label created circa 1910–1919.

Featuring the emblems of the fourteen Western states, this circa 1910–1919 label exemplifies the nation's growth during the eighteenth and nineteenth centuries.

2

PLANES, TRAINS & AUTOMOBILES

The invention of the steam engine and the advent of the Industrial Revolution sparked numerous advancements in transportation technology. The invention of the steam locomotive brought trains roaring into history in the nineteenth century, resulting in railway lines that crisscrossed the country. In 1903, the Wright brothers achieved the first successful flight in Kill Devil Hills, North Carolina. By 1909, Henry Ford was producing cars that the average American could afford. Americans, who were finding it increasingly easier to move from one place to another, celebrated these landmarks in transportation. The vehicles themselves started making an appearance on cigar box labels, not just because they were new and innovative, but in recognition that faster transportation meant faster shipment of cigars and other products nationwide.

Representative of a period of continuous innovation in vehicle design and construction, this circa 1900 automobile might be powered by electricity, steam, or gasoline. Label created circa 1900–1919.

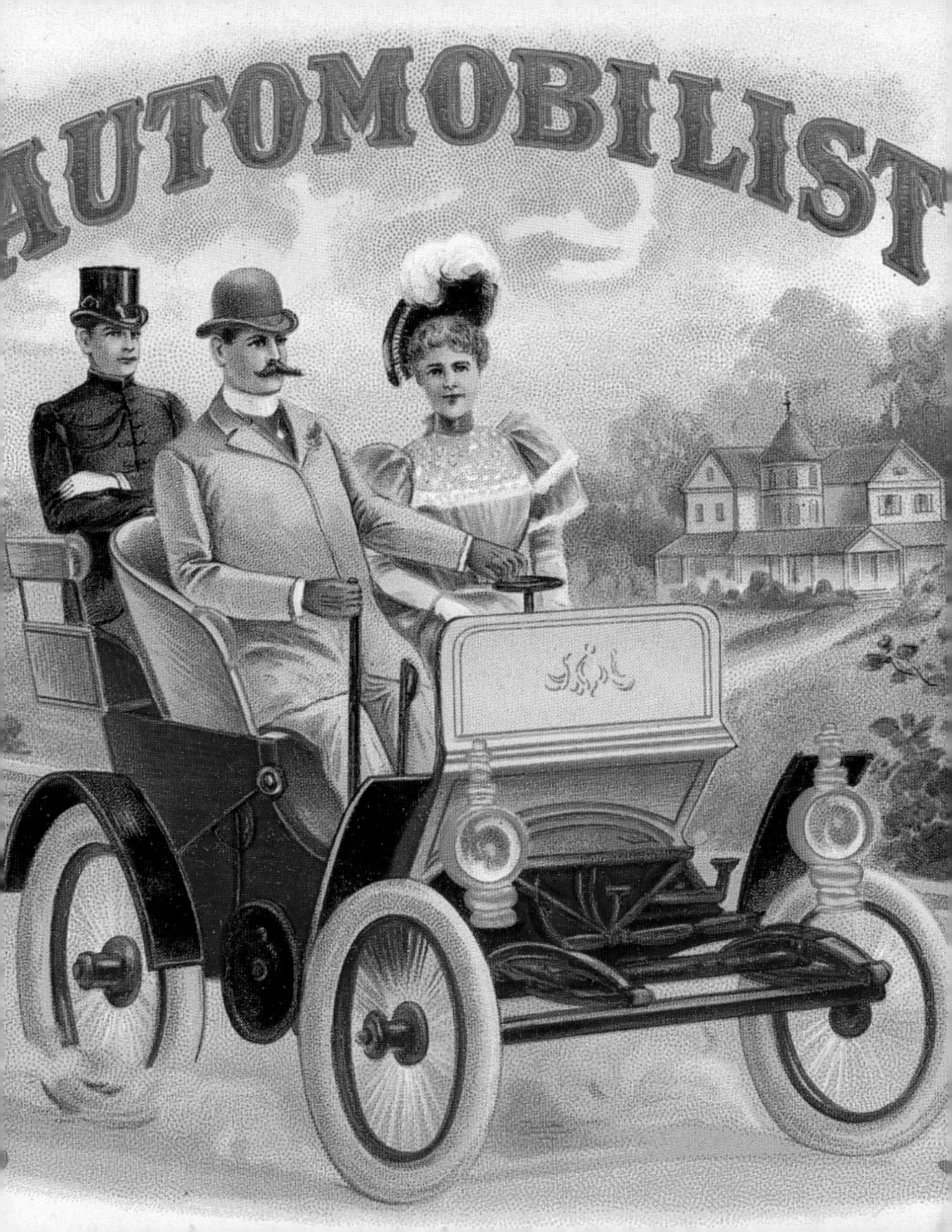
AUTOMOBILIST

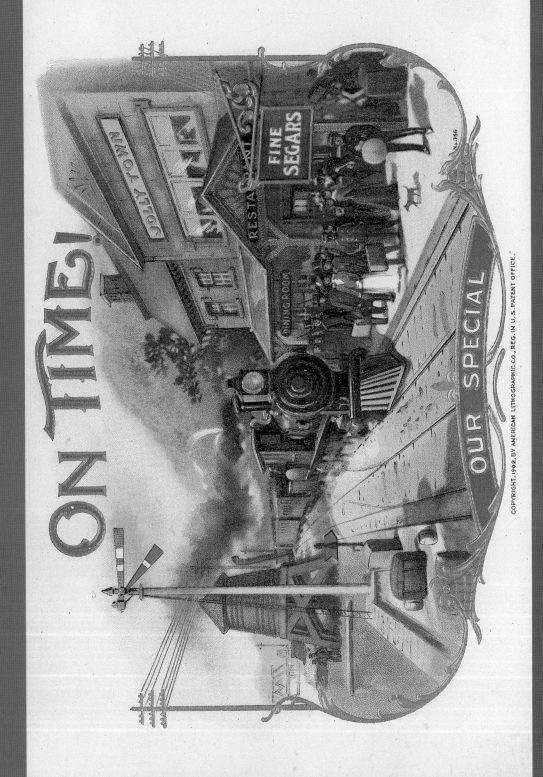

COPYRIGHT, 1902, BY AMERICAN LITHOGRAPHIC CO., "REG. IN U.S. PATENT OFFICE."

An exceptional, finely detailed railway station scene, likely made from photographic references, illustrates the period's primary mode of long-distance transportation. American Lithographic Co., 1902.

The Overseas Railroad, in operation from 1912 to 1935, was an extension of the Florida East Coast Railway added to provide access to Key West, an island located 128 miles beyond the end of the Florida peninsula at the western edge of the Florida Keys. Label created circa 1912.

Grand Central Depot, constructed on land located between 42nd and 48th Streets and Lexington and Madison Avenues, opened for business in 1871. Renovations to the depot were made at the end of the century to create Grand Central Station, illustrated on this label. From 1903 to 1913, a massive project took place on the site of Grand Central Station, resulting in the current Grand Central Terminal. Office album file copy. Chas. Stutz, March 19, 1901.

TITLE & DESIGN REGISTERED BY W.K.GRESH & SONS.

This richly illustrated circa 1900–1909 label contrasts modern mail delivery of the time (by train) with the old delivery method (by horse and wagon), emphasizing the ever-increasing speed of modern transportation. W.K. Gresh & Sons.

TRADE WINDS

BRINGS GLAD TIDINGS

TITLE AND DESIGN REGISTERED

The age of the great clipper sailing ships was long past by the time this circa 1900–1909 label was created, but the romantic image of sailing on the trade winds was carried into the twentieth century. This ship is shown sailing from Cuba to America, presumably with a cargo of Cuban cigars or tobacco.

TITLE & DESIGN OWNED BY JOAKIM ARNESEN, MINNEAPOLIS, MINN.

Part of the *Den Norske Amerikalinje* (Norwegian America Line), the ship on this 1910 label is representative of the massive ocean liners of the period. It is named after Leif Eriksson (circa 970 to circa 1020), the first explorer of Norwegian extraction now accorded worldwide recognition. He reached North America nearly 500 years before Columbus and is often named as the first European to set foot on those shores. Title and design owned by Joakim Arnesden, Minneapolis, Minnesota.

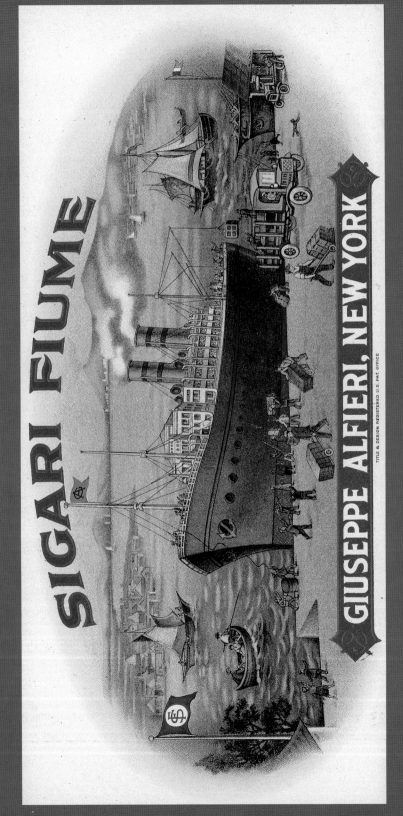

SIGARI FIUME

GIUSEPPE ALFIERI, NEW YORK

TITLE & DESIGN REGISTERED U.S. PAT. OFFICE

The massive ship illustrated on this circa 1930–1939 label appears to be powered by a steam engine. During the end of the nineteenth century and into the twentieth century, steam-powered ships provided the fastest method of oversea transportation, supporting the nation's import/export business.

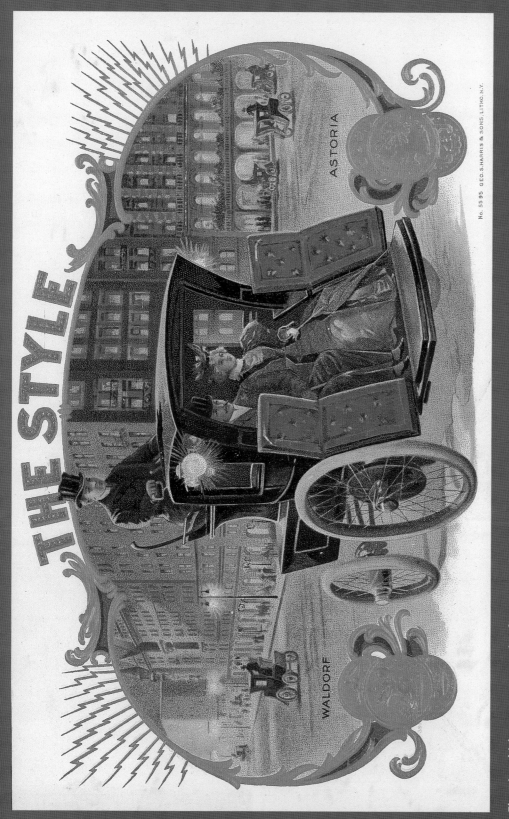

Electric vehicles arose as a mode of transportation in Europe in the late 1800s. American interest in the electric automobile developed during the 1890s. They were popular among the well-to-do, on display here, particularly as city cars. George S. Harris & Sons, sample label no. 5535, circa 1898.

YELLOW CAB

TAKES THE RIGHT OF WAY

TITLE & DESIGN OWNED BY E.B. STRICKLER.

John Hertz founded Yellow Cab in 1915 to make use of surplus used cars from his car dealership. He hired experts to determine which color was most visible. They declared yellow the winner, so Hertz ordered all his taxicabs painted that color. Label created circa 1920–1929.

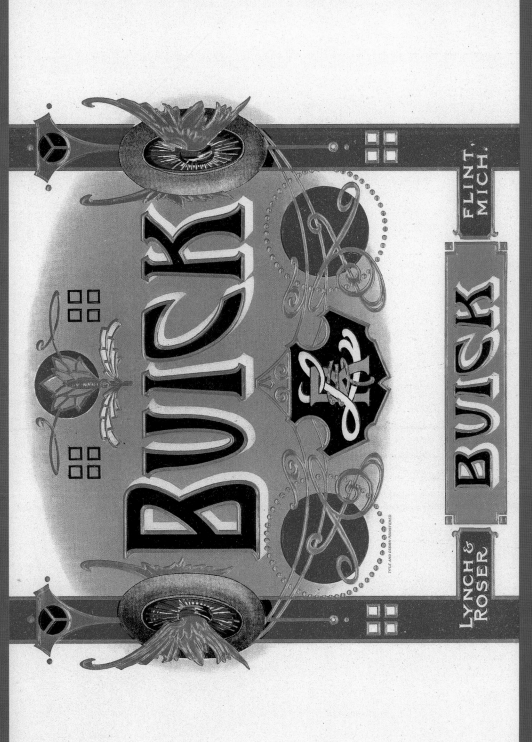

Created in the Art Nouveau style, this circa 1900–1909 label advertises Buick automobile's private brand of cigars, perhaps given to buyers or potential customers at Buick dealerships.

AERO

FIRST STEERABLE AIRSHIP INVENTED BY M. SANTOS DUMONT, A FRENCH AERONAUT,
ENCIRCLING EIFEL TOWER TWICE SUCCESSFULLY AND SAILING AGAINST THE WIND.
PARIS, NOV. 19, 1899.

This circa 1899 label depicts M. Santos Dumont, French aeronaut, successfully circling the Eiffel Tower twice in the first steerable airship, November 19, 1899.

You're Wright when you Smoke the DAYTON FLYER CIGAR

GUARANTEED STRICTLY HAND MADE AND HAVANA FILLERS

REGISTERED

Possibly known as the Dayton Flyer, the Wright Flyer III was the third powered aircraft built by brothers Wilbur and Orville Wright. Orville, situated prone, made the first flight with it on June 23, 1905, over Huffman Prairie in Dayton, Ohio. The illustrated aircraft on this circa 1910–1919 label contains two men seated upright rather than lying prone, as would have been possible in the Wrights' refurbished 1908 Flyer. Mechanic Charles Furnas flew over Kill Devil Hills, North Carolina, in the 1908 Flyer as the Wrights' first passenger on May 14, 1908.

AMERICA'S FAVORITE PASTIMES

Cigar companies were primarily trying to appeal to men with their advertising campaigns. The resulting labels reflect this, dominated by sure-fire men's subjects such as horse racing, billiards, baseball, fishing, and hunting. Card playing and similar scenes from gentlemen's clubs were also popular images, perhaps invoking the idea that a wealthy man of leisure could not relax and enjoy himself without his favorite cigar.

During the nineteenth century, golf arose as one of America's most popular sports, leading to the founding of the Professional Golfers' Association of America (PGA) in 1916. Both sexes enjoyed the sport, as shown by this label in which the woman is teeing off, not the man.

GOLF

TRADE MARK.

The image of two baseball players standing on the field in front of packed stands celebrates America's favorite pastime. M. D. Neuman & Co., March 2, 1900.

HANS WAGNER

TITLE & DESIGN REGISTERED BY FREEMAN CIGAR CO.

Also known as the Flying Dutchman, Johannes Peter "Honus" Wagner (1874–1955) played American Major League Baseball in the National League from 1897 to 1917, playing seventeen years with the Pittsburgh Pirates. He won eight batting titles, and led the league in slugging six times and in stolen bases five times. He was one of the first five inductees into the Baseball Hall of Fame, entering in 1936.

This circa 1910–1919 label's image may represent an American runner during one of the period's Olympic Games, such as the 1912 Olympics held in Stockholm, Sweden.

THE BIG NOISE

COPYRIGHTED BY C.B. HENSCHEL MFG. CO. 1911, MILWAUKEE, WIS.

Created in 1911, this label features a megaphone used by cheerleaders at sporting events to amplify their cheers for the crowd.

DICK WELLS

HOLDER OF THE WORLD'S RECORD. TIME. MILE. 1.37⅗.

Correctly spelled Dick Welles, the thoroughbred illustrated here held the world record for the fastest mile run on a circular track. He sired the 1909 Kentucky Derby winner, Wintergreen, in 1906. Label created circa 1910–1919.

The Turf

Since the chariot races in the Olympic Games of the ancient Greeks, horse racing has been a popular pastime. Churchill Downs and other prestigious racetracks presented aristocrats with an opportunity to show off the latest fashion trends. Label created circa 1880–1889.

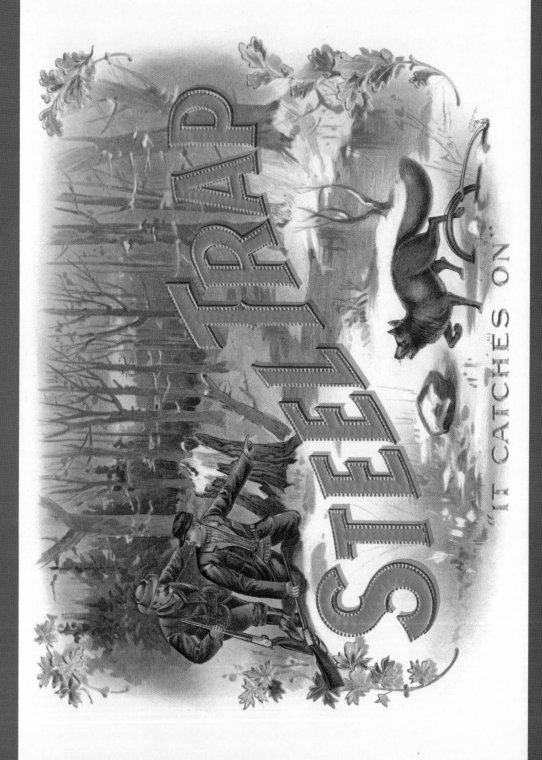

Commonly associated with trapping, a typical foothold trap comprises two steel jaws and a trigger in the middle used to spring the trap when an animal steps on it. Such traps would be familiar to hunters and trappers of the period. Label created circa 1910–1919.

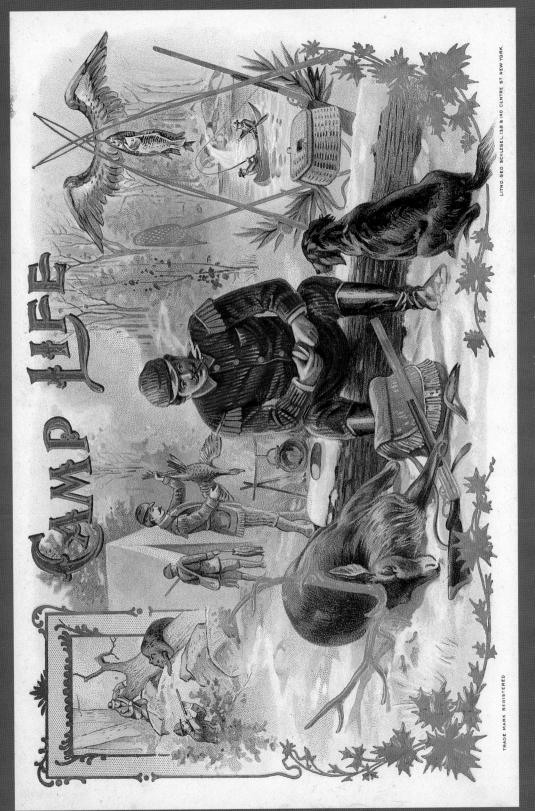

Featuring a variety of hunting and camping scenes, this circa 1890–1899 label would appeal strongly to the outdoorsman.

Richly evocative of a successful hunt, this circa 1890–1899 label would appeal to American hunters.

LITHO GEO. SCHLEGEL 139 & 140 CENTRE ST. NEW YORK.

TRADE MARK REGISTERED

A richly engraved Winchester rifle (circa 1886) dominates the foreground of this circa 1890–1899 hunting-themed label, which features gold bronzing combined with embossing.

Substituting a cigar for the shooter's bullet, this circa 1900–1909 label is sure to have been attention-grabbing and amusing to the cigar-smoking sportsman.

FISHING LINE "NO IT CATCHES"

TITLE & DESIGN REGISTERED BY GRAND RAPIDS CIGAR BOX CO.

Fishing was one of the period's most popular men's sports, and images reflecting that theme often appeared on cigar box labels. Label created circa 1910–1919.

SQUARETAIL

TITLE & DESIGN. REGISTERED.

The brook trout, also known as squaretail trout, eastern brook trout, and speckled trout, is a popular game fish. Anglers, particularly fly fishermen, would have been strongly attracted to this circa 1900–1909 label.

Developed in the late 1800s, the safety bike had equally sized wheels, a diamond frame, and a rear wheel chain drive. The bike's design made it much more stable and less likely to tip over than its predecessors. In addition, the safety bike allowed unmarried couples to go out without a chaperone. Label created circa 1890–1899.

Gentlemen's clubs in America likely sprang from the traditional British gentlemen's club. These clubs provided a place for men to gather and socialize apart from their other obligations and responsibilities. Card playing and other forms of gambling were popular among club patrons. Label created circa 1900–1909.

The illustration on this circa 1890–1899 label presents a genteel game of billiards in a men's club as an African American servant approaches with drinks and more cigars. Such a scene was likely familiar to cigar smokers of the period.

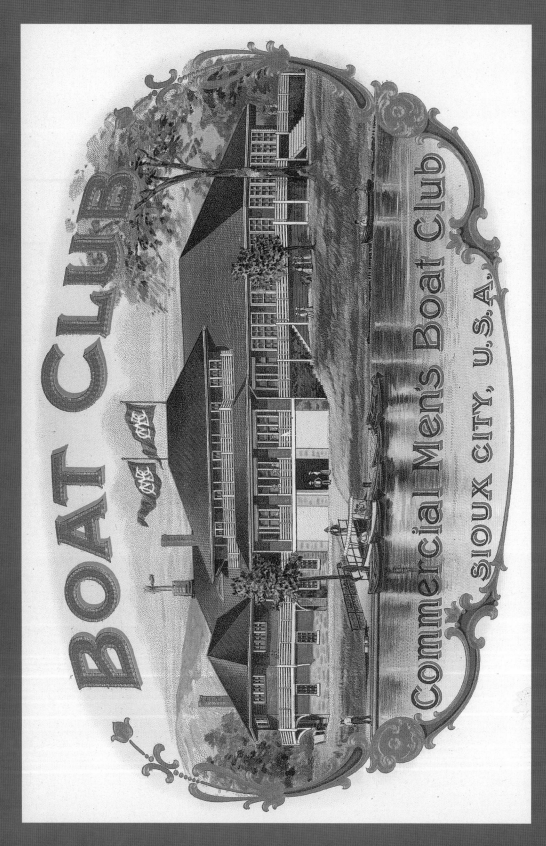

This boating club is presumably in Sioux City, Iowa. Such clubs were popular during the end of the 1800s and into the 1900s as rowing grew to be a prevalent American and international sport. Label created circa 1900–1909.

Typically, yacht clubs awarded membership only to yacht owners as opposed to those who owned smaller sailing vessels. Catering to the wealthy, who could afford such vessels, these clubs were often prestigious and exclusive, maintaining a well-defined racing program and hosting regattas. Label created circa 1890–1899.

4

A SALUTE TO THE U.S.A.

Topical subjects, such as presidential campaigns with patriotic label designs suitable for both the Democratic and Republican slates, were created to help the small cigar maker reach a broader market. These were the days before any true national cigar brands, so whatever it took to stand out from all the others was considered the main challenge in creating a salable label. Some of the imagery now seems quaint, naïve, even odd. Along with presidential campaigns, other patriotic motifs were commonly used, such as the American flag, popular presidents, war generals or heroes, and naval warships.

Abraham Lincoln (1809–1865) served as the sixteenth President of the United States. Growing up on the Western frontier, his experience building rail fences and clearing land made him an adept axman. This background allowed Lincoln to present himself as a common frontiersman, hard worker, and man of the people during his successful 1860 campaign to win the Republican nomination for the office of President. Office album file copy, Hull Grummond & Co., July 18, 1896.

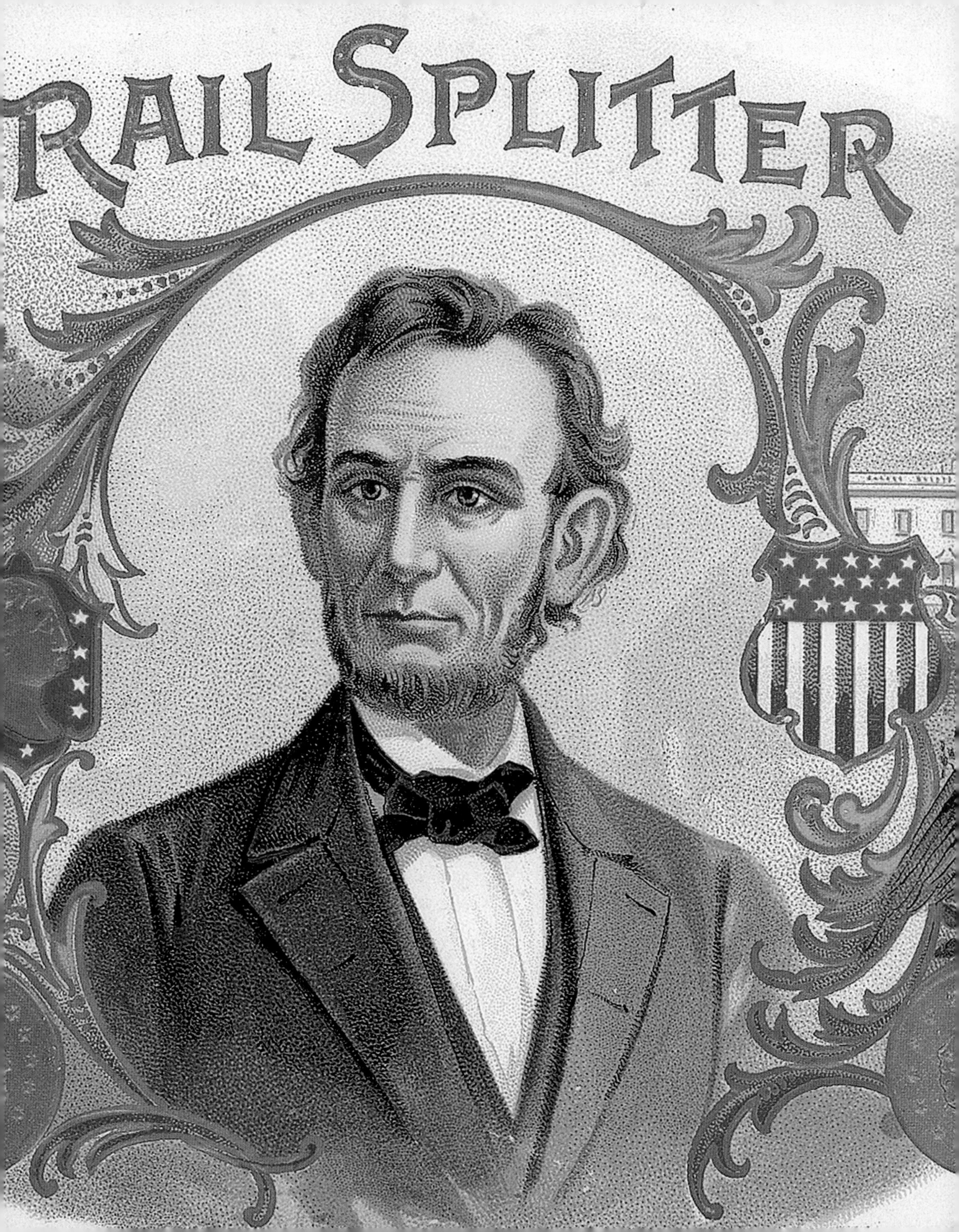
RAIL SPLITTER

LITHO. GEO. SCHLEGEL, N.Y.

THE FIRST AMERICAN FLAG

Featuring an image of the country's first flag, this label pays tribute to Betsy Ross. Office album file copy.
E. E. Kahler, February 20, 1909.

Paul Revere

MANUFACTURED FROM VUETA ABAJO TOBACCO.

TRADE MARK REGISTERED.

Paul Revere (1735–1818), silversmith and patriot in the American Revolution, set out on horseback on his famous "midnight ride" from Boston, Massachusetts, to Lexington, Massachusetts, on the night of April 18, 1775. His ride alerted patriots of the movements of the British Army. Label created in 1904.

MONTICELLO

THE HOME OF THOMAS JEFFERSON.

TRADE MARK REGISTERED BY SIMON BATT & CO.

Thomas Jefferson himself designed the house at his estate, Monticello, which is just outside Charlottesville, Virginia. Construction started on the building in 1769 and was completed in 1784. From 1796 to 1809, the house underwent renovations according to new plans from Jefferson, which called for the remodeling and expansion of his original design. Label created circa 1910–1919.

GREATER UNION

TRADE MARK REGISTERED BY B. F. & CO.

Selected as the emblem of the United States in 1782, the bald eagle, shown flying in front of the Statue of Liberty, makes an especially attractive symbolic patriotic design on this circa 1910–1919 label.

EL FUTURO

TRADE MARK.

LITH.O. GEO. SCHLEGEL, N.Y.

"The Future" presents an allegorical scene of the freeing of the slaves and the promise of their future. Office album file copy. Chas. Stutz, April 1902.

TRADE MARK REGISTERED BY RUHE BROS. CO.

Northern Civil War General Ulysses S. Grant and Southern General Robert E. Lee are featured here, along with two smaller battle scenes. Office album file copy, Ruhe Bros. Co., April 1902.

The images of three well-known nineteenth century naval officers, Commodore Matthew C. Perry (top left), Admiral David Glasgow Farragut (bottom left), and Admiral John Grimes Walker (right), surround the central image of a U.S. Navy vessel to form this circa 1910–1919 patriotic label. Made for a box of one hundred cigars, the label is larger than most.

ROOSEVELT LIGHTS

Theodore Roosevelt

Twenty-eighth President of the United States, Theodore "Teddy" Roosevelt (1858–1919) is noted for his energy and enthusiasm, progressive reforms, and strong foreign policies. Entering the office at age forty-two, Roosevelt was the youngest President in U.S. history. Label created circa 1900–1909.

"Liberty Loan" refers to Liberty Bonds—special war bonds issued by the United States Government in 1917 and 1918 to support the Allied cause during World War I. The bonds introduced the concept of debt securities to many citizens for the first time. Bonds are still used today as part of the financial and investment markets. Label created circa 1920–1929.

REGISTERED IN U.S. PATENT OFFICE

DOUGHBOY

Although theories regarding the origin of the word abound, in recent history "Doughboy" referred to members of the American Expeditionary Forces in World War I. Later, the word became an informal term for any type of American soldier. Label created circa 1910–1919.

5
WHO'S WHO IN CIGAR BOX LABELS

In addition to sports and patriotic themes, famous people and fictional characters were also popular cigar box label subjects. The notable individuals who appeared on the labels did not have to be current celebrities either—cigar box labels included many foreign and historical celebrities. Smokers of the period were apparently enticed to buy cigars with cigar-box portraits of Archimedes, Nerva, Tiberius, Seneca, Louis IX, Richard Wagner, Chopin, Liszt, Socrates, Edmund Burke, Gladstone, Jules Verne, Tennyson, Victor Hugo, Emile Zola, Ibsen, and Cervantes. Notable women such as Joan of Arc, Queen Marguerite, Maria Stuart, Marie Antoinette, and Lady Curzon were all portrayed. These figures must have meant something to the Victorian-Edwardian male to warrant the full chromolithographed treatment. The beginnings of familiar advertising themes can also be seen, such as the portrayal of famous men and women on the labels, with or without their permission, suggesting product endorsement and use. Even Queen Victoria appeared on the labels, and she hated cigars.

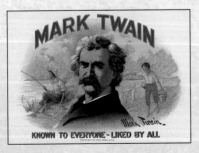

Popular author Samuel Langhorne Clemens, better known as Mark Twain (1835–1910), was an inveterate cigar smoker. His best-known novel *The Adventures of Huckleberry Finn* was published in 1884. Label created circa 1920.

REGISTERED BY SULZBERGER-OPPENHEIMER CO.,LTD.

Dante Alighieri (1265–1321), shown here, was an Italian poet of the Middle Ages. He is best known as the author of *The Divine Comedy*, an epic poem describing his journey through Hell, Purgatory, and Paradise. The poem is often considered one of the greatest literary works. Label created circa 1910–1919.

TRADE MARK REGISTERED

LITHO. GEO. SCHLEGEL, N.Y.

SHAKESPEARE

World-renowned English poet and playwright William Shakespeare maintains preeminent status in the realm of literature. His plays have been performed around the globe in countless languages and have provided some of the most popular literary quotes. Label created in 1907.

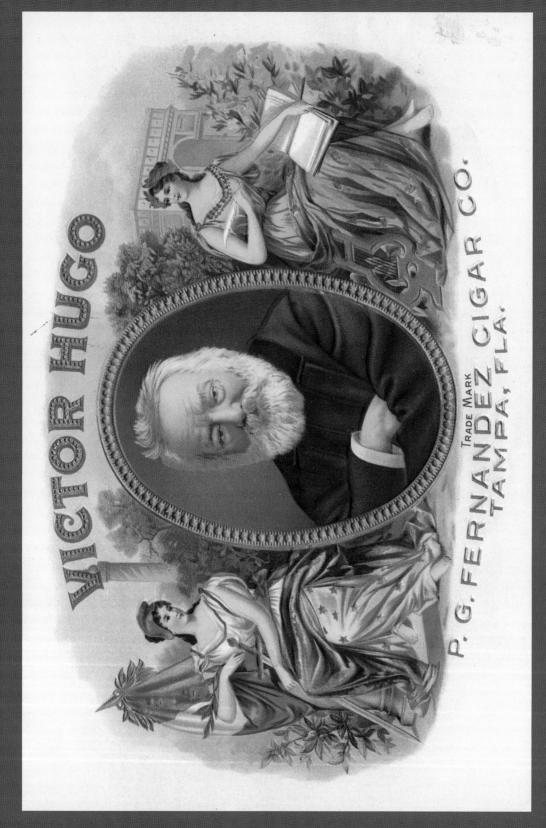

Best known for his literary works *Les Misérables* and *The Hunchback of Notre-Dame*, French writer Victor-Marie Hugo (1802–1885) stands as the central image for this 1908 label.

TRADE MARK & DESIGN OWNED BY ROBERT KLEK.

Austrian composer Wolfgang Amadeus Mozart (1756–1791) produced more than 600 works, his earliest compositions written before he turned 5. One of the most popular Classical composers, his appearance on this 1918 label is not surprising.

Joan of Arc

TRADE MARK REGISTERED

Canonized by the Catholic Church in 1920, Saint Joan of Arc or The Maid of Orleans (circa 1412–1431) is a patron saint of France. Claiming to be urged by visions of saints and angels to aid Charles VII gain the throne of France, the young girl led the French army in several key battles against the British during the Hundred Years' War. Captured, she was burned at the stake when she was nineteen. Office album file copy. United Cigar Manufacturers Co., May 24, 1907.

Featuring the images of several European queens, this circa 1890–1899 label names Queen Victoria of England (1819–1901) the "Queen of Queens."

"OPERATOR"

LITHO. GEO. SCHLEGEL. 138 & 140 CENTRE ST. NEW YORK.

TRADE MARK REGISTERED

Thomas Alva Edison (1847–1931), inventor, scientist, and businessman, holds 1,093 patents. His inventions include the electric telegraph, the phonograph, and the carbon filament light bulb. Label created circa 1880–1889.

LIEUT. ROBERT E. PEARY

Rear Admiral Robert Edwin Peary (1856–1920) is credited as the first person to reach the geographic North Pole, arriving on April 6, 1909. Label created circa 1900–1909.

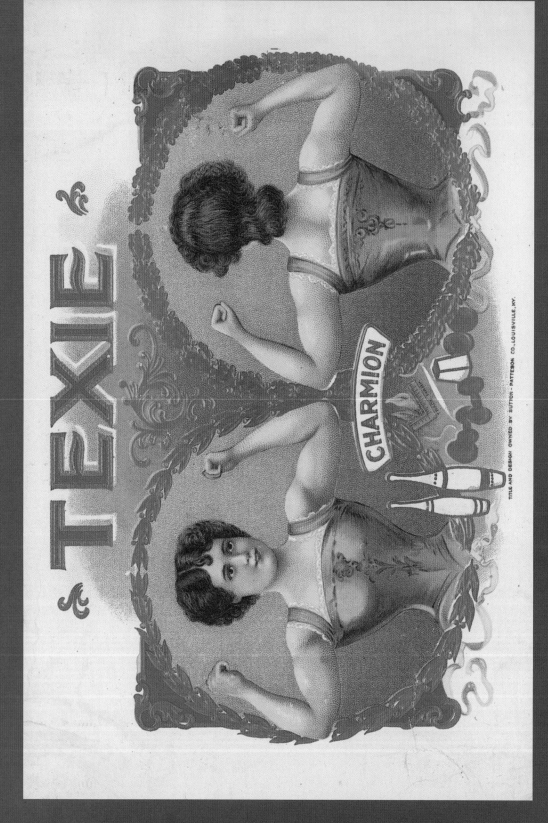

Laverie Vallee (1875–1949) was a trapeze artist and strongwoman who went by the stage name Charmion. While her trapeze act involved incredible feats of strength, she is most known for disrobing on the trapeze—going from a set of Victorian street clothes down to her acrobat leotard. The origin of the title "Texie" on this label is unclear, as Vallee was from Sacramento, California. Detroit Lithographic Co., 1898.

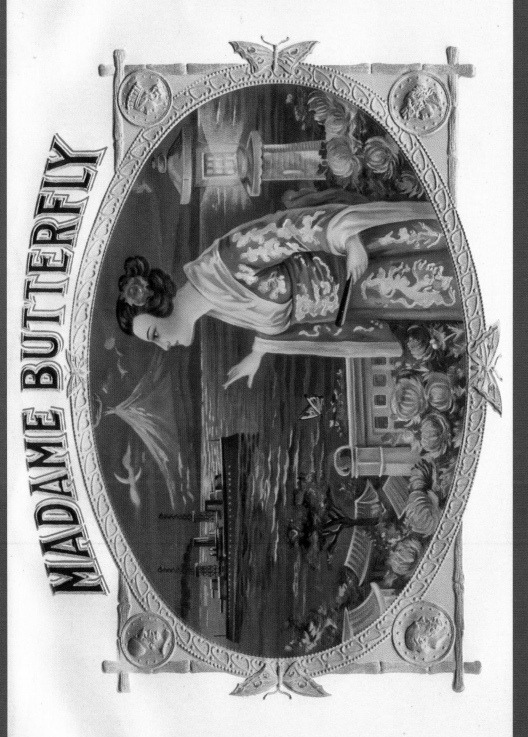

MADAME BUTTERFLY

Composed by Giacomo Puccini, the opera *Madame Butterfly* premiered in Italy in 1904 with little success. The revised version of the opera, presented several months later, received great acclaim. It is among the most performed operas in the world. Label created circa 1900–1909.

TRADE MARK

Siegfried is the third of four installments that comprise *The Ring of the Nibelung* opera by Richard Wagner, a work inspired by Norse mythology. Shown on this circa 1910–1919 label is a scene from Act II, during which Siegfried slays the dragon Fafner.

Robin Hood appears as a character in English Medieval folktales and has since grown as a literary and film character. The most popular image of this outlaw portrays a highly skilled archer and swordsman, accompanied by a group of "Merry Men," who takes from the wealthy to provide for the poor. Label created in 1912.

Lalla Rookh is the heroine of an Oriental romance of the same name published by Thomas Moore in 1817. The romance features Moore's poetry gathered into four parts to tell the tale. Label created circa 1890–1899.

COPYRIGHT, 1896, BY R.F. OUTCAULT

Mickey Dugan, more popularly known as the Yellow Kid, was a feature character in *Hogan's Alley*, a comic strip created by Richard Felton Outcault (1863–1928) and printed in the *New York World* from 1895–1896. The Yellow Kid appears on this 1896 cigar label, which was drawn and signed by Outcault.

6

THE ANIMAL KINGDOM

Some cigar labels include fantastic animal artwork. Many of these animals can be connected to the male-dominated pastimes, such as moose for hunting or the depiction of a cockfight. Dogs were often used in domestic scenes, perhaps invoking the image of the smoker as a family man. Companies also used animals as symbols to send a message about the cigars they were selling. For example, a company might utilize the royal peacock to indicate its cigars were high-end products. Finally, animals could be used to illustrate the brand name, such as Bull Durham, Monkey Brand, or Owl Cigars.

A cigar is cleverly incorporated into the design of this richly colored label. Office album file copy, H. Plagemann, August 15, 1898.

BUTTERFLY

Created circa 1910, this showcard advertising chewing tobacco features a bull as a play on the company's name, Bull Durham.

The image of an owl suggests Owl Brand cigar smokers are "wise" in their cigar selection. The use of the latest 1905 runabout automobile also indicates they are fashionable and up to date. Showcard created circa 1905.

MONKEY BRAND

TRADE MARK REGISTERED

The monkey on this August 28, 1900, label matches the name of the cigar brand it advertises.

TITLE & DESIGN REGISTERED BY DAVENPORT CIGAR BOX CO.

LITHO. GEO. SCHLEGEL, N.Y.

KING MOOSE

Moose are the largest species in the deer family (Cervidae). The large antlers on the one illustrated mark it as a bull (male). This circa 1900–1909 label relates to the brand name and would also appeal to hunters.

GOPHER

THE FOLEY BROS. GROCERY COMPANY

"Gopher" is likely a pun playing on the words "Go for." This circa 1905 label urges customers to "go for" the Foley Brothers' private brand of cigars at their grocery stores.

The image of a royal peacock on this circa 1905 original watercolor art for a label design plays on the word "regent," while also suggesting the brand is high-end.

ROYAL PHEASANT

Native to China, the male Golden or Chinese Pheasant has colorful plumage and is a popular game bird. Its appearance on this 1905 label might suggest this brand's cigars are exotic.

This circa 1900–1909 label presents a scene typical of a cockfight, a popular form of entertainment. The fighting birds also hint at the fierce competition for sales among cigar companies.

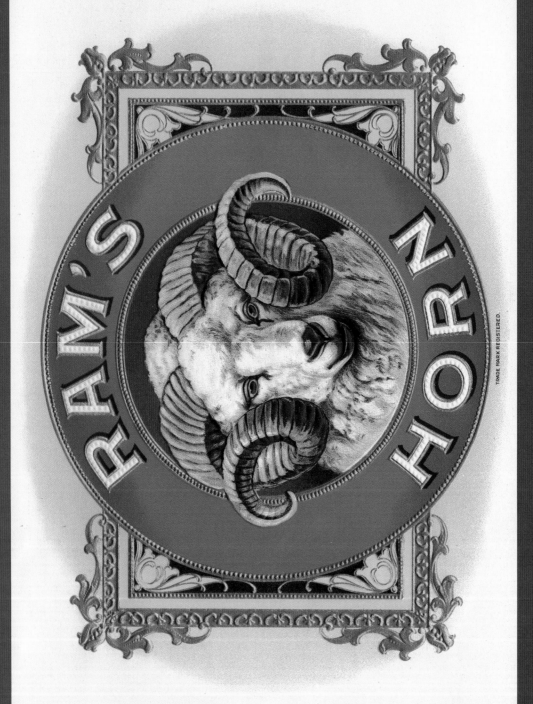

TRADE MARK REGISTERED.

A play on the cigar's name, this circa 1910–1919 label displays a male Rocky Mountain bighorn sheep. A bighorn ram's horns can weigh up to 30 pounds (14kg), and the sheep itself can weigh up to 300 pounds (136kg). The ram's image adds a masculine association to this cigar brand.

Greetings to Dad

MAN TO MAN

ROI·TAN

THE CIGAR THAT BREATHES

A special occasion label, this circa 1950–1959 advertisement utilizes the conventional image of the family dog fetching slippers for the man of the house. Of course, this dog also brings a box of cigars. Altadis U.S.A. now owns the Roi Tan brand.

The striking image on this showcard presumably represents the proud, successful, and confident smoker of Tampa cigars. Showcard created circa 1905.

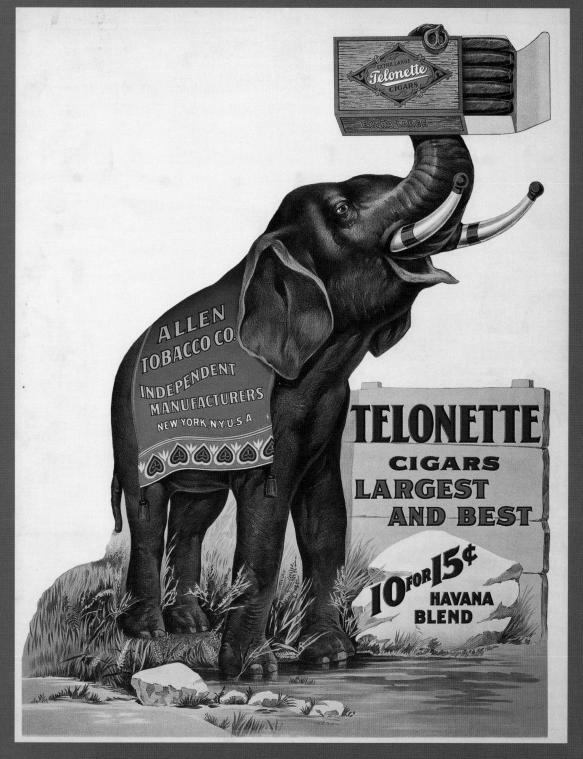

An elephant appears on this circa 1905 showcard proof as the only animal capable of lifting the "largest and best" cigars.

7

JUST FOR A LAUGH

Some labels were made to attract customers by appealing to their good nature. These featured humorous images, such as Moses and Uncle Sam lighting up or slightly risqué or silly scenarios. Customers would pick up the box of cigars because the image made them chuckle and would hopefully like the cigars so much that they would keep coming back for more.

Only a few labels featured religious figures. This tongue-in-cheek image invites customers to enjoy a cigar worthy of such a holy individual. The label's title plays on a colloquial exclamation, in this case expressing amazement and wonderment over the great smoke of the cigar. Label created circa 1880s.

JOLLY MONK

LITHO. GEO. SCHLEGEL, N.Y.

TRADE MARK REGISTERED

Surrounded by images related to beer and wine, this smoking monk has clearly moved away from strict self-denial and is partaking of some worldly pleasures.

N·O F·L·I·E·S ·O·N M·E

TRADE MARK REGISTERED

LITHO GEO.SCHLEGEL 136 & 140 CENTRE ST.NEW YORK.

Possibly a reference to Eugene Field's poem "Jest 'Fore Christmas," the phrase on this label suggests smokers of these cigars are quick-witted and intelligent. Label created circa 1880s.

A bizarre label image, this coin-pinching bug might indicate these cigars are high-quality *and* have a great price in an attempt to appeal to more thrifty customers. Label created circa 1910–1919.

Risqué images of women often appeared on cigar box labels as cigar companies sought ways to appeal to their primary customer: the American male. The woman in this label is a heated representation of a fireman's fantasy.

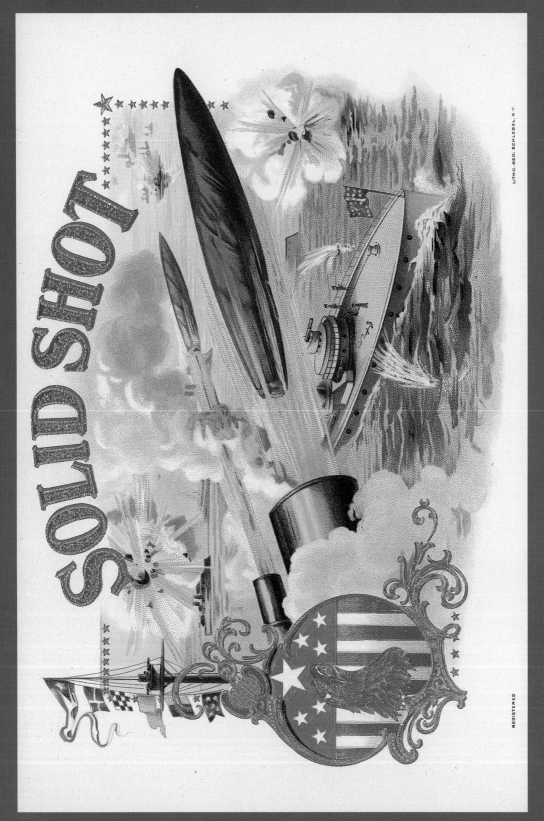

The image on this circa 1900–1909 label portrays a stirring visual gag on the shape of cigars, while the text indicates the certainty of a great smoke. The design may have originated in an earlier edition during the Spanish-American War.

SWEET LIBERTY

UNCLE SAM:===="WELL I DON'T KNOW!"

This somewhat wizened Uncle Sam chain-smokes his favorite brand of cigars, but it seems he can't determine whether the cigars are domestic or imported. Office album file copy, United Cigar Manufacturers, April 1909.

The title on this playful label has a double meaning, suggesting the tobacco in the cigars is also full weight, with no filler added.

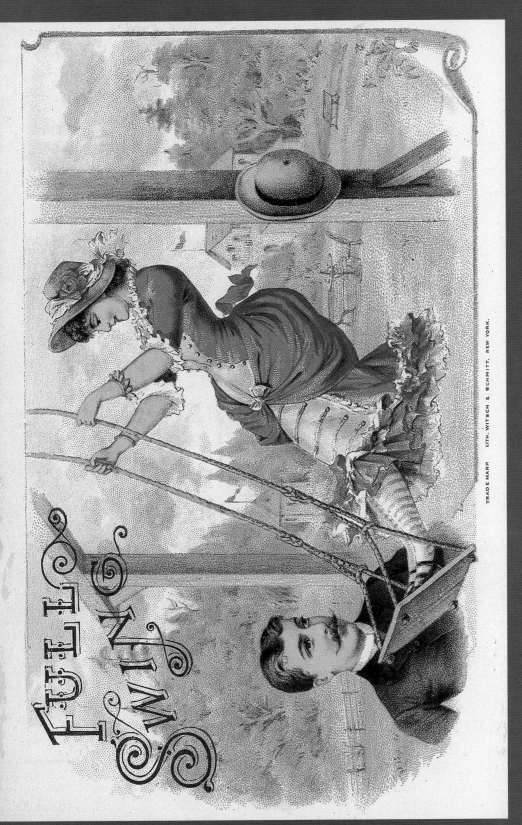

This playful image shows a young man catching a scandalous glimpse of a woman's ankles. Witsch & Schmitt, circa 1880s.

8
GRAPHIC ART

Early cigar box labels were frequently conceived as full illustrations in the manner of narrative painting popular in the academies and the salons. As time progressed, the full rectangular format began to be superseded by an oval shape containing the illustration with the title in relatively modest lettering. A further significant design change came in the 1890s when the lettering became bolder and ornate, enhanced with ornamental flourishes, gold accents, and embossing. Following the ascendancy of the cigarette in the 1920s, the number of cigar brands and variety of imagery began to severely diminish, as the repetition of a brand name was found to be more critical than image variety. Large, simple, bold lettering within equally bold color panels, non-pictorial subjects, and heavy emphasis on the brand name characterize this style. After the war in the '50s, Contemporary Modern and graphic artists arrived with flat simple colors and shapes and the generous use of white space.

Featuring a striking contemporary Christmas design, this 1955 label was created by well-known graphic designer Paul Rand, who utilized the product itself for inspiration. Altadis U.S.A. now owns the El Producto brand.

The snowman on this circa 1910–1919 label seems to be presenting a box of cigars as a great holiday or Christmas gift.

This bright, attention-grabbing circa 1910–1919 label has an odd title. Perhaps it concerns some topical subject involving turkeys at the time.

The state flower of both Mississippi and Louisiana, the magnolia has long been associated with the southern United States, and this label may have been intended for that market. It is also possible the manufacturer of this graphic 1900 label may have been located in the South.

COPYRIGHT 1927 BY PENNSYLVANIA CIGAR CORPORATION

Reflecting the later style of design for cigar box labels, this label focuses heavily on the brand name and displays the product larger than life. Label created in 1931.

9

EVERYDAY AMERICA

Ultimately a cigar company had to appeal to the average American male to make sales. Consequently, scenes from everyday American life often appeared on cigar box labels. Images of college students, working men, and popular topical subjects were placed on cigar box labels in the hope that their familiar appearance might appeal to the average man. The labels might also incorporate period inventions, like Thomas Edison's phonograph or Cyrus McCormick's reaper.

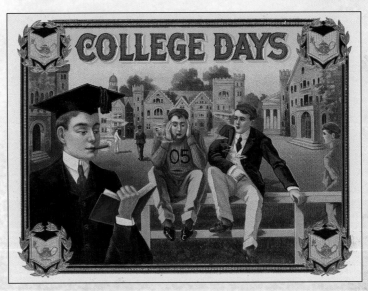

This college scene would have been familiar and appealing to members of the upper class who could afford such an education. In addition, college students likely presented a good market for cigars. Label created circa 1910–1919.

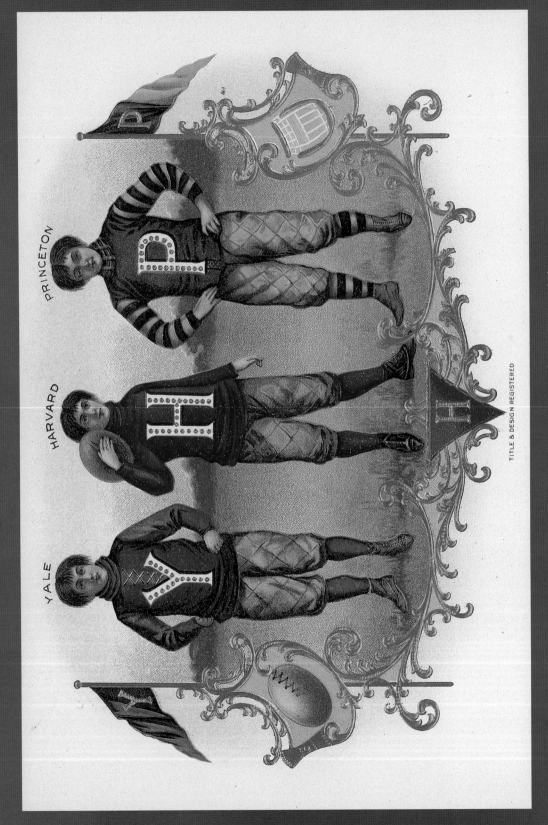

TITLE & DESIGN REGISTERED

The original version of this label, created by the Paul I. Landmann Company (Mannheim, Germany) circa 1905, featured three European rugby players. The label was updated in the 1920s by the George Schlegel Lithographic Company to feature three rugby players representative of Yale, Harvard, and Princeton.

TITLE & DESIGN OWNED BY HERMAN JACOBY.

Vassar College was founded as a private women's liberal arts college in 1861 in Poughkeepsie, New York. In 1969, the college started enrolling male students, becoming co-educational. The portrayal of an early women's basketball team on this circa 1900–1909 label is noteworthy—basketball was played at the college starting in the late 1800s.

Queen of the Ring

This label bursts with the excitement of the circus, a popular attraction. The bareback rider presents an image sure to capture the male cigar smoker's attention. Louis E. Newman & Co., sample label no. 844, circa 1885.

TWO FRIENDS

TITLE & DESIGN REGISTERED

The idea of owning a dog for companionship instead of as a working animal grew more popular throughout the nineteenth and twentieth centuries. This circa 1910–1919 label plays on the concept of man and dog as friends and might also serve as a subtle affirmation that the cigar and the smoker are friends.

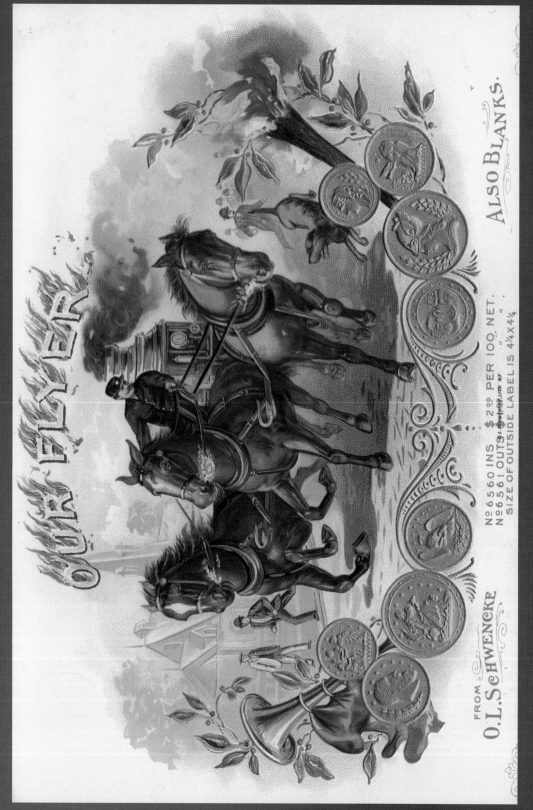

Created circa 1895, this label captures the excitement of thundering fire horses pulling an American steam fire engine belching smoke. O. L. Schwencke, sample label no. 6560.

EDSONIA

IT SPEAKS FOR ITSELF

TRADE MARK REGISTERED

LITHO. GEO. SCHLEGEL, N.Y.

Thomas Edison filed for a patent for the phonograph in 1877. His design featured a needle that indented vibrations from speech into a tin foil cylinder. Later improvements on Edison's design included use of a wax cylinder, such as the ones shown on this circa 1900–1909 label.

McCORMICK'S HARVESTER

EXTRA QUALITY
FINEST BINDER

TITLE & DESIGN REGISTERED BY J.L. McCORMICK

Inventor of the mechanical reaper, Cyrus H. McCormick (1809–1884) would have been a household name for American farmers. In 1847, McCormick established a factory in Chicago to produce his reaper. The factory grew to become the McCormick Harvesting Machine Company, now McCormick International USA, Inc., one of the world's leading suppliers of farm equipment. Label created circa 1920–1929.

THE LOGGER

LITHO. GEO. SCHLEGEL 138 & 140 CENTRE ST. NEW YORK.

TRADE MARK REGISTERED

This circa 1880s label advertises a workingman's cigar.

In 1817 a group of stockbrokers formed the New York Stock & Exchange Board, later shortened in 1863 to the New York Stock Exchange. The group had already been in operation since 1792, running under the Buttonwood Agreement, which set out the rules they used to properly buy and sell bonds and companies' shares. Label created circa 1900–1909.

TITLE & DESIGN REGISTERED

This label illustrates the popular terms "bear market" and "bull market" used to describe the stock market. A bull market indicates a period of hopefulness as prices of securities rise, while a bear market indicates a period of falling security prices and doubt. These terms are perhaps connected to each animal's characteristics—bulls being depicted as energetic and bears as slow and lumbering—or their style of attack—bulls attacking with an upward thrust of their horns and bears attacking with a downward swipe of their paws. Wm. Steiner, Sons & Co., circa 1900.

LITHO GEO SCHLEGEL, N. Y.

TITLE & DESIGN REGISTERED BY WOHL & COMSTOCK CO.

Individuals who had just paid off a mortgage would enjoy smoking one of these cigars. Those with an interest in financial subjects might also purchase a box. Label created circa 1910–1919.

INDEX

ACQUISITION EDITOR: Peg Couch & Alan Giagnocavo **COPY EDITORS:** Paul Hambke & Heather Stauffer
COVER & LAYOUT DESIGNER: Jason Deller **ASSOCIATE EDITOR:** Kerri Landis **EDITOR:** Katie Weeber **INDEXER:** Jay Kreider

More Great Books from Fox Chapel Publishing

Labeling America
ISBN 978-1-56523-545-8 **$39.95**

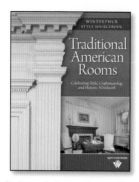

Traditional American Rooms
ISBN 978-1-56523-322-5 **$35.00**

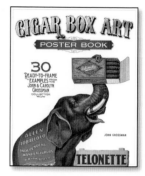

Cigar Box Art Poster Book
ISBN 978-1-56523-743-8 **$24.99**

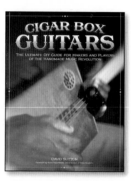

Cigar Box Guitars
ISBN 978-1-56523-547-2 **$29.95**

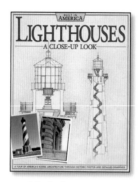

**Lighthouses:
A Close-Up Look**
ISBN 978-1-56523-560-1 **$19.95**

History of Lovespoons
ISBN 978-1-56523-673-8 **$14.95**

Learn to Play the Ukulele
ISBN 978-1-56523-687-5 **$14.95**

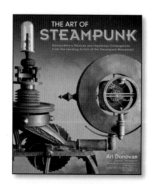

The Art of Steampunk
ISBN 978-1-56523-573-1 **$19.95**

Handmade Music Factory
ISBN 978-1-56523-559-5 **$22.95**